PROMETHEUS BOUND

derived from Aeschylus

Prometheus Bound

Robert Lowell

FABER AND FABER   *London*

First published in England in 1970
by Faber & Faber Limited
24 Russell Square London WC1
Printed in Great Britain by
Latimer Trend & Co. Ltd Whitstable
All rights reserved

SBN 571 09274 8

Author's note

Aeschylus's *Prometheus Bound* is probably the most lyrical of the Greek classical tragedies. It is also the most un-dramatic—one man, a sort of demi-god at that, chained to a rock, orated to, and orating at, a sequence of embodied apparitions. In translation, the poetry seems lofty and dead, and the characters statues. Something living somehow burns through even the worst translation. I took one of the dullest I could find. Seldom was there any possibility or tempta-tion to steal a whole phrase. Yet I kept the structure, either roughly rendering or improvising on each speech. Half my lines are not in the original. But nothing is modernized. There are no tanks or cigarette lighters. No contemporary statesman is parodied. Yet I think my own concerns and worries and those of the times seep in. Using prose instead of verse, I was free to tone down the poetic eloquence, and shove in any thought that occurred to me and seemed to fit. My idea was for some marriage between the old play and a new one.

I hope I will not be accused of concocting my own anarchic miasma. Most of what may be found perplexed or too vehement in my Zeus and Prometheus is also to be found either explicitly or hazily in Aeschylus. Zeus is the laws of nature, or nature's God, as the eighteenth century might say, or even a stage in Greek political evolution. He hardly lives up to his position. Is it the wisdom of Aeschylus, the pinch of plot casting, or the hallucinations of the miserable Prometheus that give Zeus the character of a hard dictator, some Tiberias, or Trujillo? Would it all have unravelled to good in the final play of the trilogy, another *Eumenides?* Prometheus in rebelling is justly fighting for intelligence and justice, or justly fighting against necessity, or he is *un*justly fighting, because he is fighting necessity, what is. These confusions and insights are in the archaic plot, much as they are in Milton's, and are irreconcilable with reason only if one wants to translate the old myth into marching orders.

Characters

FORCE

POWER

PROMETHEUS

HEPHAESTUS

THREE SEABIRDS, THE DAUGHTERS OF OCEAN

IO

HERMES

The première of *Prometheus Bound* was presented on May 9, 1967, by the Yale School of Drama at New Haven, Connecticut. The play was directed by Jonathan Miller, and sets and costumes were designed by Michael Annals. The cast, in order of appearance, was as follows:

Prometheus	KENNETH HAIGH
Drummer	STEPHAN MILLS
Attendant	JEROME ANELLO
Force	EV LUNNING
Power	BRETT PRENTISS
Hephaestus	CLAYTON CORBIN
Three Seabirds, the Daughters of Ocean	LAURINDA BARRETT
	JOAN PAGE
	JOAN WEISBERG
Ocean	DAVID HURST
Io	IRENE WORTH
Hermes	RON LEIBMAN

PROMETHEUS BOUND

POWER

We've reached the end of the road, the topmost stone on the rooftop of the world.

FORCE

Beyond here, everything is downhill.

HEPHAESTUS

You've hauled Prometheus here; you've done your job. Not a very kind or subtle job, but who thought you had talents for a painstaking gentleness? Go home; you're not needed now; go back to your stonebreaking and volcanoes. You can go, but I must stay here, and give my finishing touch and binding-knot to your labors. Prometheus is a god . . . yes, we gods also have our loyalties. Shall I imprison him in endless winter? Oh, I suppose I will do it very willingly. I can be twisted as easily as my own burning metals. Each step I take tells me what it is to go against Zeus. I didn't go very far. My Father straightened me out with his thunderbolt. Crooked legs learn to walk a straight line. (*Turning to* PROMETHEUS) Oh, Prometheus! You know that I act as much against my own will as yours. Here are your chains, here is your rock. No hand will loose you. You will never hear the voice of man. Here, your flesh, that frail flower, will wither and go black under the rays of the all-healing sun. You will hate the sun, and yet night-long you

3

will pray for sunrise to dim the cold simmer of the stars, and melt the frosts of morning. Each day will bring you the fertile heat of summer; each night, the barren cold of winter. Every season, every month, and each minute in each hour will tell you that your present suffering is the worst you can live through. Time will tell you that you must live through worse.

Even though you were a god, you weren't afraid of your fellow gods. Now you and this rock have come together. Now you stand upright—like twins, one rock, knee and neck unbent, the sentinel of the world. You still stand because you have to stand. But Zeus stands because he wants to. Cruelty is his form of courage. (*Exit* HEPHAESTUS, *limping as before, but still more slowly*)

POWER

Prometheus, you can't move an inch now, can you? Your hand is finished with solutions. From now on neither action nor sleep will interrupt your thoughts—only thought following thought in a desolate downward spiral. Night and day, you will think with relentless stubbornness, and only on one subject: your suffering. Now and then, perhaps, man and the benefits you brought him will enter your mind, but no man will ever hear you, see you, or lighten your pain. No man is strong enough to climb here. No man lives long enough to finish this journey. It's laughable that you are called Prometheus, the Foresee-er. As long as the rule and order of the world remain, you will foresee only what you now see: Force: this rock unchanging, yourself unchanging, Prometheus unchanged and chained to this unchanging rock. (*Exit* FORCE *and* POWER)

Prometheus Bound

(*Alone*) Bright sky, bright sky, bright sky! The wind is up, and strikes my face. I hear waterfalls foaming down the mountain drops; miles lower, I hear the endless gnashing laughter of the waves dying out on the sand. Everywhere below me, the inescapable earth. Above me, the inescapable sky. The sun on its stiff rounds—nothing overlooked, nothing understood! So helpless here, anything living can hurt me. Under this blank sky, nothing will open.

Wait. I hear something, a whirring of birds. The air is sinewed with their fragile wings.

> [*The stage lightens. Women dressed like gulls slowly revealed everywhere. Then, as the gulls fade away, three gulls come forward. Their harsh voices are sometimes accusing and sometimes comforting, though the comfort may often seem harsher than accusation.*]

FIRST VOICE

We too are helpless, or almost so. We were perched on our nests in the sea-caves, thinking of you, unable to forget. Then the sounds of some blind force hammering at your chains vibrated through our rocks. We knew we must come to you.

SECOND VOICE

We came to our Father, poor, tired, quelled old Ocean. He sat weeping for you, stunned and drifting with his tides, less able to move at his own will than the sea about him, yet he gave us his watery permission to rise.

THIRD VOICE

At first we were carried upward by the breezes. Soon we

5

left them behind. We left your wife, Alcyone, behind. She had no urgency. We left her, a dot of blue, fussing with the strings of her sandals, lost in the distance.

PROMETHEUS

My wife is coming; yes, I can hear her light footsteps rattling the small stones on the trail. Her pity for me has made her lag. Hurry back to her, warn her she mustn't come yet . . . The wings of the hawk are too freshly smashed, his eye is frightened and starved.

FIRST VOICE

Alcyone is delaying.

SECOND VOICE

She hasn't made up her mind to set out yet.

FIRST VOICE

Because she loved you once, she only wants to remember you in glory.

THIRD VOICE

She never leaves her island now.

PROMETHEUS

Who gave her an island? Was it Zeus?

SECOND VOICE

Zeus knows well from experience how possessions refresh the grief-stricken. He gave Alcyone an island to rule.

THIRD VOICE

He wished to spare her the torment of idleness and loss.

PROMETHEUS

So, Alcyone only wished to remember my glory! She will never look at me. . . . Others rebelled and were more fortunate. They rebelled, they were buried. Now they hardly hump the curve of the earth. He who looks for them will not find them. He who looks for me will see me and learn his lesson.

FIRST VOICE

We are afraid of these new gods. Their claws are already changing to hooks, yet none of them will look up at you, Prometheus, and rejoice. Your chains are too close to them. Only Zeus aspires to be beyond fear. He cannot rest from trampling on chaos.

SECOND VOICE

Zeus cannot sleep until he has planned the destruction and torture of a friend.

FIRST VOICE

Who knows anything about God, except that his ways are dark and very seldom pleasant.

PROMETHEUS

He is dark to others, and darker still perhaps to himself— not all darkness, though. When Zeus no longer knows his mind, or can see his hand, he will reach for me. And I . . . what can I do but welcome him?

We cannot see that time. Tell us, if there's no harm in telling, why you are here and what you have done.

PROMETHEUS

I have done many things . . . What brought me here? Everything I am brought me here. The good old days. They were never good. We come from a snake wrapped around a mud-egg. We have struggled to where we are by living through a succession of tyrannies. Each ended when the cruel wisdom of the serpent had been broken by the formless mud, each ended when a son cut down his father. Then Cronus, the Father of Zeus, came. Now that he is gone, we look back with regret on all the evil he didn't do, but he was never a good king. Half the gods wished to throw him down. My brothers, the Titans, were on the side of Cronus. They were very strong and very stupid. They stood about shining and sharpening their spears, and boasting that they would throw heavy stones farther than anyone had thrown them.

I went to Cronus. He was a bad and easygoing god, a lump of mud and aches dressed up in a helmet that didn't fit, but he liked to talk. "I want your advice," he would say, and then keep on talking. He remembered everything he'd ever done. He seemed to take a kind of pride in his failures to rule. "It's all so hopeless," he'd say with a laugh. "I wouldn't change a thing I've done. I'd do it all over again." I saw the head of Cronus was a slab of meat, and it seemed to me if I could cut through the slab of meat, I would find a silver ball. The ball was there, it cracked open, inside it another, and another and another, and then suddenly, the

8

head of Cronus, my own head, and the heads of all the gods were broken spheres, all humming and vibrating with silver wires. The whole world was an infinite sphere of intelligence. "There's a mind in things," I said to Cronus. Cronus went on talking. I went to my brothers, the Titans. They went on shining and sharpening their spears. "If you or anyone else bothers us," they said, "we will pick up a volcano and throw it." Courage was easy for them, the old gods, but the least thought a torture.

FIRST VOICE

We know you went to Zeus then, but why did you betray your brothers?

PROMETHEUS

I couldn't help myself. I had to choose between the destruction of my brothers and the betrayal of my own mind. It was worse than death then, stupidity rising and wallowing above us, like a tide of mud, all of us choking, all of us shouting at once—I too choking and shouting, but still able to think and warn. But no one heard me—no one! Then Zeus listened. What glorious days then, what a quick and lovely instrument Zeus was! He had only to lift his finger and whole armies of Titans sizzled under volcanoes. Advising him I was the mind of the world. I was the mind of the world! No, Zeus is the mind of the world—and the hand! I was; Zeus is!

SECOND VOICE

Why did Zeus chain you to this rock?

Zeus had to make nothing of me, so that he himself could be everything. That's the law and disease of tyrants—they are more sensitive than we are . . . If a friend makes a slip, they see a traitor. But is Zeus a tyrant? I'm not sure. He cut through things at first. Each god was given his place and function; no more overlapping offices. He was, and still is, I think, a good enough god for the gods. Man was what troubled him. Zeus looked at man with disgust, and said, "Why do I put up with man? He cares for nothing except dirt, blood, and sex? He is always the same. He gets nowhere. Why don't I wipe him out?" When I heard Zeus, I said to myself, "Poor man, the king of the gods hates you. None of the gods will help you. Perhaps, if you have fire, you can help yourself." So, man has fire! And Zeus, the inscrutable, has not wiped him out, but has consented to let him live, miserable, dying, though equal to the gods in thought. I . . . I have been punished. I thought I could move the world. Now the world moves, I stand here, another obstruction, another dark spot in the merciless perfection of Zeus.

FIRST VOICE

But why do you stand here in chains? You haven't told us.

PROMETHEUS

I gave the sufferers a drug. Now they often forget about dying.

SECOND VOICE

How was that possible? What drug?

PROMETHEUS

I gave them hope, blind hopes! When one blind hope lifts, another drifts down to replace it. Men see much less surely now, but they suffer less—they can hardly draw breath now without taking hope.

THIRD VOICE

What more could you give men after this consoling blindness? Perhaps you wished to let them go on living forever. I think you gave them something more terrifying.

PROMETHEUS

I gave them fire.

FIRST VOICE

Another drug! Another blind light.

PROMETHEUS

Used skillfully, fire can remake, or destroy the earth. Man's uses, however, are limited—a few inches and minutes to crawl along a plank sticking out from a cliff. The plank ends, and near the end, there is always some victim standing fixed like a nail in the wood.

FIRST VOICE

This death, this walking off into nothingness, won't go on, will it, when God, each day growing more at ease with men, and less concerned with them . . . Then God will have proved himself.

God may get used to man and lose interest, but gods never believe they have proved themselves. I am afraid of the blind ambition and helplessness of God. Suppose he is powerless to pardon, and only almighty in his power to inflict pain? Mmm? I see a little into the future. Oh voices of the sky and ocean, if you will stop darting, if you will be quiet, if you will sit at my feet . . . I will try and lighten the sorrows that I and the gods have made you feel. Sorrow and misfortune wander at will through the air, a cutting edge, yet always a glitter. No one escapes the attention of God.

FIRST VOICE

We will come nearer, Prometheus. Though we are not permitted to stand in any place or position long.

> [*Music, swan-sounds, enter* OCEAN, *the father of Alcyone,* PROMETHEUS's *wife, the father and source of all birds. He is a tall, fat god with a beautiful white curling beard—good-natured, but now and then, vexation and venom animate his great languor.*]

OCEAN

This poor, old fading flesh . . . No, Prometheus, you mustn't fatigue me with your apologies. Don't accuse yourself for standing rooted here, and letting me run hither and thither for you. Look at me as the dust under your feet, another stepping stone for your ambitions, another rung in your ladder. When you married my daughter, and began to rise each day in the esteem of Zeus, I was proud of you.

Then when I heard of your imprisonment—how you like to surprise us!—I never thought of my own safety. Careless of my own life, I came running to your side. Yet these seabirds, my children, are here before me. Young wings, sure wings! I fear these creatures are closer to you than their mother and father. . . . Wait! I can't see well . . . I must wipe the sweat from my eyes. You've made me rush so . . . Yes, I was not deceived. Alcyone, my dearest daughter and your wife, is not among them. Well, she was always discreet, and now she has her own great responsibilities. She is ruling her own house now. She still treasures your glories. Now you are encircled by seabirds, all wing and motion—no staying power. I'm surprised they have left the haven of their waters. No, I remember now, I myself sent them on ahead. "Birds of the sea," I said in my grief and confusion, "sail on before your father, the ocean. Steer onward to Prometheus, sound out the rocks and reefs." A few of them might have stayed behind, and helped me on my journey. I've lost momentum on this uphill climb. Prometheus, my son, you're not listening, you are looking at my poor right arm. Don't give it a thought. It's only paralyzed—bent hard and stiff as a fish-hook. That's from managing and buffeting with this big bird. Now here we are at last, swan and rider, both winded, both letting our wings and arms flop—a sad pair of ambassadors. Clever of me to harness a swan. Quite an invention—like one of yours, Prometheus. Sometimes, he got out of hand. Birds aren't horses. I guided him with my mind. No reins or bit. A telling word, a timely touch, that's my strategy. That's why I am still carefree and youthful in my old age. Be friendly, try persuasion—never use the bit.

PROMETHEUS

I see you have weathered your journey, but I am surprised you have the courage to stay and talk. You are risking your life.

OCEAN

Blood is thicker than water. Your father-in-law still has duties and privileges. No, you are mistaken . . . I haven't come to beat off these birds. My children's whims are sacred. I think their shrill voices are beginning to grow on you. (*Steps back, continues more formally*) Prometheus, we are saddened, amazed and appalled by your punishment. Even if we weren't related, I would be here. No one has so earned and won my respect, my affection. I don't know whether to call you my son, or my brother. You used to be my son. You know I am speaking the truth. Prometheus, I say to you, "I am here. Use me!"

PROMETHEUS

No, you'd better go back. I see your eyes are hurt by the glare of these rocks, you don't like to stand in the open. Already you are furtively glancing over your shoulder, as if you longed for that dark rabbit-warren of rock-roofed caves I helped you to build. There's no diving under water here. This place is dangerous.

OCEAN

Zeus knows where I am. On my way here, I felt the heavy shadow of his gaze. I shivered, yet knew the full weight of God's power, and wish supported me upward to my goal.

14

This journey to your rock was no spontaneous and idle impulse. I might almost call myself the emissary of God. I think I am free to tell you, that Zeus still feels a sort of nostalgia for those distant days when you and he fought side by side against the criminal chaos of Cronus. All that was before your imprisonment, but I think we still have time to come to terms with God. You still have some mysterious value to him. I can't imagine . . . You are frowning. Perhaps you think I have changed my coat and wear the servile livery of the victor. "Once," you are thinking, "old Ocean found Zeus too serious about ruling." Well, I have changed. The world runs now. Zeus is gracious to me, he called me his fellow ruler, the ruler of the ocean . . . as if I were such a ruler as he, I who never wanted or was able to rule anything—I who like to lie on my back, and sway like a flap of kelp with the tide.

PROMETHEUS

So, you have swung round to Zeus. You are an emissary. It doesn't suit you. You fitted in much better with the old hit-or-miss rule of Cronus. But I was no gloomy and backward Titan. When the war was on, I never hesitated to choose sides. I was the trusted friend of Zeus. This is how he has broken me.

OCEAN

Yes, say I have come from Zeus, if you wish, Prometheus, but do not think I am happy to see you in chains. This doesn't surprise me, but I am surprised by your rash stiff words. Listen to me. If you are too subtle to understand me, I will repeat myself like an old man. My advice is know yourself, and change. You helped establish the new order, now you must live in it. You are wise, but you do not know how to hold your tongue. You stand on a height, but Zeus is far above you. He is not so far lost in his heavens that he can't hear your words. They grate on his ears like a knife on a grindstone. Soon, your torture will be far worse. You are wise, but you do not know how to surrender. You think your defiance is godlike and noble. You think my advice is too ignoble and servile to have any meaning. You do not know that I am your good fortune. I have grown old and carefree by teaching myself to give in. Your punishment has taught me, though Zeus neither teaches nor wishes to be taught. I will go back to him and say that you submit, you repent . . . yes, I have interpreted your thoughts . . . I am no ruler, but I know what rulers like to hear.

PROMETHEUS

You are at home with rulers, but you have lost touch with the ruled. I wish for those aimless and earlier days, when you used to sound me out so softly and at such reassuring length. Oh, that ocean of talk, that tropical sea washing over and over me from sun to sun—many bright fish there, many valuable weeds. In the past, lost in the rambling and dim immensity of your waters, I sometimes felt I caught glimmers of bottom, and heard the unintelligible weeping of chaos. No ebb then, no end; but now that ocean is dry. I wonder how you dare rebuke me. We shared the same hopes. Something might be done, you thought, if fire could be given to man. *Something could be done!* Nothing weighed on the buoyancy of *your* hopes.

Prometheus Bound

OCEAN

Dreams, Prometheus. Our hopes were noble exercises for the mind. Why did you put them into action?

PROMETHEUS

I have done what I have done. I suffer. I knew I would suffer.

OCEAN

Still unchanged, still ungoverned, Prometheus. Still giving advice, still unheeding. Yet who needs help more than you, or less than I? I am almost the soul of reason . . . Prometheus, why do you rob me of my reward? Do not send me back to my cave, where I can only hear the damp echo of my own voice.

PROMETHEUS

You have changed. You are now an echo of power, a soft echo rolling back and forth between tyrant and victim, explaining tyrant to victim, and victim to tyrant . . . always explaining and softening, an echo that no longer understands what it echoes. You wish to serve, and yet be at your ease—an impossible ambition under Zeus. Others as ill-prepared as you have tried to deal with Zeus. Some tried submission. Remember my brother, Atlas, the strongest of the Titans and the most patient. Atlas was submissive. He obeyed Zeus like an ox. Now Atlas bulks by Gibraltar, and holds the world on his shoulders. If he flinches—so Zeus has persuaded him—the world will fall on him, and break him. Perhaps, in the end, you too will have to try rebellion. My brother, Typho, was rebellious. He had his hour. By his own will, Typho crawled on his hands and knees from the great ooze—once ooze himself, later a monster topped with a hundred heads. He thought no god could stand up to his murders and ugliness. He was immovable. He squatted in one place, hissing out smells and terror from his hundred mouths. More mouths than the gods could count, he thought. All his eyes gave out a sickly yellow glare. "I am the death of the world," he said. "Let Zeus look on me, and die." Zeus looked. The unsleeping thunderbolt hit Typho, then flames went for his heart. He had only one heart for his hundred heads. When he looked at himself—he looked at himself with his two hundred starlike eyes—he was frightened. He lay like a bed of ashes on the ground—no stir, no breath, except the heavy, descending stifle of his smell on the air. He will lie long now by the narrows of the white-toothed Mediterranean under the spurs of Aetna. And Hephaestus, a kind god as the gods now go, will sit on the cone of the volcano. Hephaestus's eye will be beady with zeal, as he shovels burning lava on Typho. Yet Typho has some hope, he won't be altogether useless and inactive there; from time to time, he will be allowed to hiss and gasp a little, then his ashes will burn the Sicilians and their fields. Many deaths, many deaths, many fields turned to solid stone! Yet the Sicilians meant nothing to Typho, who had nothing against their harmless vineyards.

OCEAN

Do not compare me with Typho. I have never threatened the gods with a hundred eyes. I only drift and talk . . . a little too much perhaps, but no one was ever much harmed or changed.

PROMETHEUS

Yes, you were wise and cautious when you came here. You will be still wiser and more cautious when you leave. Rebellion was never a great temptation for you.

OCEAN

I must return to my ocean. When I am there, I will remember this mountain, and our old hopes, those noble and inconsequential exercises of the mind, all the dearer to me, because I never hoped to improve the plans of God.

PROMETHEUS

Remember nothing. Zeus doesn't want his servants to remember. He likes to leave them free to repeat their past mistakes.

OCEAN

I am going. I will always remember you. Here, take this feather. I have already given you my seabirds. This feather is all that is left me. Take it, blow on it. Later, while you stand stock-still here suffering, the winds will tear it away. Then you will envy my flight. I must be going. My swan is impatient. The soft down on his breast already seems to ruffle for the warm airs of the down-glide. He is eager for rest and fodder, the fish and weeds of his little pond. (OCEAN *goes off on his swan. Soft mournful sounds*)

PROMETHEUS

Poor seabirds, you must be proud of your father. He sees us from a dizzying distance, sees only the harsh glinting, and blurred outlines of a great landmark. I wish I could use this

feather he gave me. Then I could fly off like a bird . . .
one day soaring feathers, the next a fluff of dry, descending waste. I would be dead before I even knew I had died.

You speak lightly of dying, Prometheus. We could never
live with the thoughts that clash through your clear mind.

Who has seen the mind of Zeus? If he thinks at all of the
gods who ruled before him, he thinks with contempt, and
is silent.

But the peoples of the earth cry out in sorrow at the down-
fall of those old powers and their long-held honors. The
Titans are gone.

O Prometheus, not only the people of the earth lament,
but the sea that bore us mourns.

Each wave tears itself apart, when it hits the shore. The
waters under the earth are black. The waters above the
earth will never stop weeping, descending and breaking.

That water is turning to ice, a fine dry snow. It dazzles me a
moment, then bites my face. I pretend I can bear it; yet I
begin to think of my enemies. Those gods! That innumer-

able jumble of upstarts, all screaming with one voice, all howling for power! Once they filled Zeus with the stupor of despair. And now? They are almost perfect. They spin about the head of Zeus—each as delicate and cold as a snowflake.

Enough. We know the gods. They watch us. I will tell you about the feverish miseries of man. Before he could reason, he was an animal, perhaps the slowest and least graceful, a skull with less inside it than the shell of a turtle. I am not saying this in scorn of men, but to show the greatness of their change. Men had eyes and saw nothing: a shapeless presence, a threatening absence, nearness seeming so distant that it hit them in the eyes, distance seeming so near, they tried to duck their heads. No finer shades! They saw little in between the blinding yellow of the sun and the blank of night. They had ears and heard nothing: a splatter, a splash, fizzings, buzzings, hissings, mazes of muddled vibration, sounds without the cutting edge of words. What did men know of houses built of brick, and turned to face the sun? They swarmed like ants, though with far less order, through a sunless underground of eroding holes. Leafless winter, flowering spring, and fruitful summer were all one season to them. The stars looked down on them like an aimless sprinkle of water drops running out into nothing.

I taught men the rising and the setting of the stars. From the stars, I taught them numbers. I taught women to count their children, and men to number their murders. I gave them the alphabet. Before I made men talk and write with words, knowledge dropped like a dry stick into the fire of their memories, fed that fading blaze an instant, then died without leaving an ash behind. Now the brute forces of the earth obey man slavishly whenever he thinks and speaks. I have put animals under his thumb—dog, cat, and cow, horses to plow, horses to saddle, horses to harness to the warrior's chariot. While the animals drudge, man sits thinking so idly and so profoundly that he can hardly be troubled to budge and sort out the wealth and luxury that drops in his lap. Men were set floating in boats, a pole to push, an oar to pull, a sail to hoist. Those windy sails . . . men thought I'd turned a block of wood into a bird!

All these inventions were given to men. Thousands more followed. I could turn anything into anything.

FIRST VOICE

You have thought too much, Prometheus.

SECOND VOICE

Feverish earth images spurt and crackle through your poor mind—so much done for man, so little for yourself!

THIRD VOICE

Man has his own doctors, none has ever been able to cure his sickness of death.

PROMETHEUS

Man's short life, when I first looked at it, short as it was, was a long disease. Man was an animal without an animal's resolution for going on. If a man sickened, he would usually die. No one mixed medicines, brought cooling drinks, or knew what food to choose. I searched the earth, and discovered it was a map of cures, covered up, mislaid, rotting, but eagerly waiting. A cure was waiting like a bride for every disease. But perhaps man couldn't have faced living out his life, if death had abandoned him.

I stopped teaching cures. I taught men to see into the future. What future they had was as close as death, but not so certain. They had dreams, some true, some false, some . . . I think I taught them which were true. They heard voices in dreams, awake, anywhere. I made men listen, then they understood what those modest seeping sounds were trying to tell them. There were signs at every step along man's way, yet he was trampling them down, and hurting himself because he couldn't read their message . . . Look, you cannot see it . . . a vulture is swinging nearer to us from the distant sky. Crooked taloned, fat, with an empty stomach—it seems to have found us out. It might be our release. Man would know; I taught him. I taught him the feuds, hungers, lusts of birds, and why they gather. I made man stare into the entrails of beasts, see their smoothness, roughness—each had a meaning—see what kind of gall would please the gods, see that the speckled symmetry of the liver lobe had meaning, the thighbone swimming in fat, the long spine jointed like these chains. Everything in animals, even their excrement meant something. Their innards would be correctly set on fire to appease the gods. I made men look into the fire. Alone and bemused in the slothful dark, they studied the fire's whirling and consuming colors, and believed they would some day taste the breath of life. No one knows, I haven't told anyone, the many wonders I have invented. I was out of my mind, my hand was everywhere. Everything man knows. . . .

FIRST VOICE

You have done too much. This hailstorm of gifts is poverty.

THIRD VOICE

Prometheus, we must suppose there is some larger order or shaping hand directing everything; even your punishment, to some outcome.

PROMETHEUS

No hand, no larger order! There was a kind of low and lifeless order before the gods existed; after they are gone, there will be an order.

SECOND VOICE

A kind of low order?

PROMETHEUS

Before Zeus, the lesser order of Cronus; before Cronus, the still lesser order of Uranus. Still less, still less, still less! An infinite whittling away. The nothingness of our beginning is hard at work to bury us.

THIRD VOICE

No, Zeus is eternal.

PROMETHEUS

Zeus eternal! Why he is counting his days. Perhaps he is already more than halfway through his count.

THIRD VOICE

You changed man from the highest of the animals to the lowest of the gods!

FIRST VOICE

Man is a poor god, too intelligent to hide from his unceasing guilt, too stupid to escape. That story trails off in death.

FIRST VOICE

This is the wisdom, Prometheus, we have learned by looking at you.

[IO *rushes onto the stage. She is large, beautiful, distracted. She has cow-horns on her head.*]

IO

What land is this? What people? You only seem to be talking. You can't speak now, can you?

PROMETHEUS

Zeus set me here.

IO

Zeus! If you were Zeus or served him, you would look at me. You would look at me closely. I am still warm and alive. A little dirtied by the air though. Do you see that smudge off there on the sky? It's the flies swarming, gathering, buzzing. Hera set them on me. They follow me, they drive me, they watch me. Oh, I had another watcher once, Argus, the herdsman with a hundred eyes. The wife of Zeus set *him* on me too. Now he is dead, but his eyes still glitter. These fat, blue flies sting me like needles. They are like the

roll of his eyes, bloated, watery-tongued. No, Argus is dead.
But there isn't earth enough to fill his hundred eyes. His
eyes are still liquid circles, they still hang and gape on that
pile of dry white bones. They glisten up at me from his
grave. I run from him. I have wounded my feet on the
shells of the sea, now I cut them here on each rock I climb.
No, I have escaped. Zeus killed Argus for me. I no longer
hear the nagging drone of his shepherd's pipe, or feel his
breath blow on my moist neck. That slippery hand . . .
It's clean now, the flies have stolen the last string of gristle
from its bleaching joints. The flies are free now to follow
the richer steam of my flesh. This heavy flesh . . . I seem
to wade through my own heaviness, as if I were a pasture
sinking back into marsh.

PROMETHEUS

Don't think of Zeus. He doesn't come here. *I* am here. I
know who you are, you are Io, the daughter of Inachus.
Perhaps Zeus loves you still, but he has grown slow of foot
and weary of the pursuit. He wants to hide from the jeal-
ousy of his wife, Hera, the cow-eyed queen of the gods. She
is driving you before her like a wild beast. She has set her
flies of corruption on you. They will not leave you, while
you wander in pain through the interminable turnings of
the earth. There's no returning to your lover now. If you
look back, you will see that the fields behind you are on
fire.

IO

My sight's steadier now. I see you are alive and a god. Not a hard god. I think you know that I have done nothing cruel, and only suffer because I was loved by Zeus. Forgive me for distrusting you. I was never very wise, even before I met Zeus. And now this fly-blown flesh, these flies . . . I know that I must suffer, because I suffer without grandeur or nobility. But how can I believe in your tortures, or in anything that can be done to the great? I have seen too many of your huge brothers bubbling in bogs, spitted on crags, fuming under volcanoes. Such great acts of vengeance are all so extreme and alike. I thought the victims felt no more than a forest when it is burning, or a rock when it is crumbling. When I first came here, I was still light-headed. I couldn't believe in you when I saw you standing up against the high, thin, disabling air of this mountaintop. I was almost ready to laugh at your icy splendor, these chains as big as cables, these brilliant red drops of blood, and this savage rock. Forgive me, I thought this was another majestic example of punishment that Hera had thought up to drive me mad. Hera, or one of the gods, or even Zeus, because I sometimes think his mischievous and uncanny mind plans and consents to everything that has been done to me. You can think. I think you must know everything. Tell me where I must go, and how long I must keep running. Who are you? How do you know my name?

PROMETHEUS

I am Prometheus. Yes, I know you . . . that had to be . . . knowledge was once my affliction. Come nearer, Io, I see the gods have changed you.

Don't look at me, Prometheus. Don't think of me. These cow-horns . . .

PROMETHEUS

Oh, long before I saw you, Io, I was thinking deeply about you. The thoughts of God were open to me then. I saw he thought only of you. No, I wish he had; he thought of other things. You and I were burning and burning together in the mind of God, I in his anger, you in his heat and anger.

10

I never saw you before, Prometheus.

PROMETHEUS

Nor I you, Io. We were only together in the mind of God, in that radiant and malignant mind. Come nearer. I won't be eloquent or subtle or harangue you. I think I can learn from you. You show up a weakness in Zeus. He can fall in love.

10

No one will ever fall in love with me again, now that I am swollen, and half-changed to an animal, a cow.

PROMETHEUS

You still stand back. You stare at me in fear.

IO

Yes, I think you see everything I have done or will do.
Help me.

PROMETHEUS

You see what my foresight has done for me.

IO

I know you helped the dying creatures. I am one of them. I
never wished to be more, but tell me why we suffer.

PROMETHEUS

Why do we suffer? My concentration on suffering will
never end. I am too tired. I see only the surfaces of things. I
see you, Io, but not with the eye of Zeus.

IO

Don't look at me, only tell me something I want to ask you.
It's about you, not me—something ugly and meaningless to
me.

PROMETHEUS

What are you asking?

IO

Who nailed you here, and why?

PROMETHEUS

Hephaestus drove these nails home. Do you see that chip of
iron lying at my feet? It smashed off his hammer. Hephaes-

tus is no more than that, a hammer in the hand of power, a smashed chip of iron.

10

How can Hephaestus be only a thing? Even under the eye of Zeus, the under-gods have their rules and rights. They are not like us. They have wills. They do things because they want to. Why was Hephaestus willing to nail you to this rock?

PROMETHEUS

Why? These servants of Zeus . . . they are like polished bronze balls with spikes on them. They grind us, they crush. We have laws; God alone has motives.

10

I must leave this rock.

PROMETHEUS

You will leave it soon enough; then a long time later, you will bear a child to Zeus. Then you will leave the earth, and the earth's dry crust will forget how it bruised your feet. Those who knew you will forget even sooner how they hurt you.

10

I could not stay here as you do. The flies and my fears would force me to break these chains. When I leave, when I die . . . perhaps the gods will let the flies crinkle up and die. They too must want to give up sometimes. Where must I go, Prometheus? How long must I trample on the earth?

PROMETHEUS

Do not ask me where you are going. The road goes nowhere. Why should I show you that round of repeated steps? Perhaps you would like to count them. No, pray for the narrow brain of a cow, and its thick leather hide.

IO

Where am I going, Prometheus?

PROMETHEUS

Many places, many places. You'll be lucky, if you know nothing about them beforehand, and forget them when they are gone. Pass them . . . I want to spare you . . . without looking and on the run. Think of the peoples of the earth and their dwellings as no more than the clouds of dry brown dust stirred up by your feet, and settling behind you.

IO

What I imagine for myself is more frightening than anything even the gods could dream of. Why do you keep putting off my questions? You said I would bear a child.

PROMETHEUS

Yes, that will be near the end.

IO

You are afraid to look ahead. That's why you are chained

here. Prometheus, look at me, and speak the truth, if you can.

PROMETHEUS

When I close my eyes, I am able to think, I can almost move. In the darkness, the stars move down on us like burning metal.

IO

Are you thinking about our deaths?

PROMETHEUS

Our deaths! No, Io, even yours is less close than you might wish. . . . Listen, far off somewhere, somewhere trapped in time, I hear the monotonous flapping of a fly's wings.

IO

At least you hear something alive.

PROMETHEUS

No, this fly is only bringing death closer, as it flaps or wraps itself in what will kill it—some syrupy ooze or the dry threads of a spider.

FIRST VOICE
Stop, Prometheus!

SECOND VOICE
You are threatening us like Zeus!

THIRD VOICE
Don't teach us!

FIRST VOICE
Everyone knows about death.

PROMETHEUS
Zeus too is flapping his torn wings perhaps. Tyrants drowning in their ooze like to catch at the lines of love.

FIRST VOICE
Empty mutterings!

SECOND VOICE
Zeus will long outlive the loss and death of Io.

THIRD VOICE
Don't you know that even now we are in the hands of Zeus?

PROMETHEUS
If I could die like Io, I would be free. I don't want to be God. God is only able to kill.

FIRST VOICE
Your words won't kill Zeus. I think they will only stir him to kill us!

THIRD VOICE
Listen to Io.

You needn't listen, Prometheus, if far and near, past, present, and future are the same to you . . .

SECOND VOICE

You see what you don't see, you feel what no one feels.

THIRD VOICE

We are different. We hunger for what is close to us.

PROMETHEUS

You were young, when Zeus came to you?

10

The house of my father, Inachus, Prometheus . . . you must know it, it's the best house in Euboea, and has the largest herds. There, a little before now . . . no, long before . . . just before my mother's death . . . I was born, another human lump, without shape or strength or the heart to crawl. The fields came close to me then, and cattle followed the fields, and the herdsmen seemed to lean on the shoulders of the cattle. And when men and animals changed places to look at me, I looked back at them with their own dazed, absent-minded stare—ribs rising and falling together, one soothing sound of tooth and tongue and crunched stalk . . .

Then I learned to walk, and was allowed to follow the cattle. I went out with them at sunrise, came home with them at sunset. I could speak to the cattle. Later, I could speak to the herdsmen. Later, I could speak to my father . . . Animals, servants, and my father, their king—they went on looking at me with the same look of coarse, indifferent kindness. I might have been a boy, or a calf . . . Then one morning, I saw my father in a thundercloud— no, not my father, but a face with splintered black eyebrows, a beard of black rope, and a smile, obscene and royal . . . the face of Zeus. Lightning flashed at me from the cloud, like the wink of a man, and I knew what the god desired. From then on, even in the clearest weather, the cloud would stand above the fields, and wait for me. My father's servants couldn't scare it from the sky with their sticks. Then I began to scream at it. I was led home, and shut in my room.

I was told the cloud still stood above the fields for days and waited. Then at last, thundering and roaring and whimpering to itself, it ran off like a wolf. That night, I saw Zeus, still cloudy, but darker and made of flesh now. I felt my breasts rise, and grow hard, I couldn't take my eyes off the god. I pitied him too, because he was thin and black, and looked scorched to the bone with his despair. His hands smoothed and soothed me. His black, swollen lips brushed my skin. His tongue slithered and slimed in my mouth. My thighs unclenched. I heard the voice of Zeus, saying, "Io, your time has come. Our time has come." Then a crash of thunder—God was gone. I was unhappy. I felt a flatness. I missed my lover. When I reached out for him, I saw Hermes, the messenger of the gods, standing by my bed, and waving me back with his wand. "Io," he said, "I have come to join you in marriage with the highest power." Then I pitied Hermes, because he seemed young and tense and unused to such missions. His armor was like armor that had never been worn, and not a feather on his wings was out of place. Hermes said, "Zeus is on fire for you, Io. Don't you hear the impatient grumbling of his thunder? Hurry. We must leave this house, its molding would smother Zeus. Come with me. The great pasture of your father will be the marriage-bed of Zeus." . . . I remember that walk—hot brown grass like an oven under my feet, excited cattle, nudging against me, and rolling up their eyes. At every step, I felt the slow swish and slap of a tasseled tail. The air was thick and rich as hay. The whole pasture lay like a huge panting body. Then I saw Zeus. He seemed to say, "Take me. I must rest from my labors." Then I looked at the cattle and thought to myself, "These creatures do not take life, or frighten anyone. I will be like them. They have never resisted the gods." Then I became like them, I became God's creature, and Zeus, for a moment, had his rest in me.

PROMETHEUS

Zeus found his rest in you, but you had none.

10

No rest, no sleep. I hid in my room—no sleep there, only drawn-out hours of half-sleep, soiled and ruffled by my guilty visions. Tongues sticking to my tongue. Rough hands chafing at my breasts like the sands of the desert. At all hours, the bellowing of animals, their tails curling between my legs, the watery, seductive gurgle of their throats, their thick tongues saying, "Go to him. Go to him." I was changing, I was growing larger, I was with child. Each new swelling of my body was terrible and painful to me, but I thought Zeus needed me, and I tried to go to him. Then

Hermes came again. His armor was disheveled and comfortable on him now, and he spoke with an easy arrogance, as he blocked the doorway like a veteran soldier, and chewed the tip of his wand. "Io," he said, "stay where you are. Have pity on Zeus. He will not be pleased when he sees how you have swollen." Then I fell. When I woke, I saw a woman sitting by my bed, and I thought she was my old nurse, because she was brown and wrinkled and healthy, and because she was soothing my head with a cold cloth. But it was Hera, the wife of Zeus, and she was bending close to me and singing, "Sleep, my child. I give you a day and a day, and perhaps another day, to gather your strength. Then I must never let you rest." My eyes had red splotches on them, and the pain made Hera's face tremble a little menacingly in the heat, but soon the room was still, and I saw that Hera was doing her best to be gentle with me, and was even trying to brush off two flies, as big as her thumbs, that had crawled from my swollen stomach, half-dead, and already beginning to mate. "Don't bother with these flies," the wife of Zeus said. "When you see them again, they will be a thousand. When women are warm enough to make love, the gods send them flies. The flies rise from your sticky flesh, are warmed by your heat, and kept alive by the blood from your thighs or the milk from your breasts."

I went to my father. He kept looking off in the distance, and counting on his fingers, as if he were counting his herds. I said, "I have been visited by Zeus." My father didn't hear me. He went on counting on his fingers. Then I said, "I am with child by Zeus." Then my father heard me. In his madness, he struck me, and even sent out men to beat the hills for the criminal. Then he sent messengers to the oracles at Pytho and Dodona. They answered darkly. "Give Io air. Let her breathe. Knock holes in your walls. Tear the roof from your house." My rooms were torn open. All day then, I was looked at by the cattle and the herdsmen and my father and the gods and the winds. The holes were like eye-holes in a skull, and Zeus seemed to be watching me through the eye-holes. Then the oracle spoke more clearly. "Give Io air. Give her the world. She must leave her father's house, and run across the earth and never stop running until she dies. If you try to hold your daughter back, the fire of God will destroy your house and your herds and your kingdom."

Then I began running, and my mind grew small and hard. Horns began to push through the side of my head. They hurt at first, but the swelling of my stomach stopped, as if my child had stopped growing. Then I thirsted, and forgot my horns and my child, and the gods let me wade in the slow sweet stream of Cerchnea, and drink from its pools. No flies were pursuing me then, but the wife of Zeus had already sent Argus, her herdsman with a hundred eyes, to watch me. At each bend in the river, I would see Argus sitting on the bank and dangling his feet in the water. He would play pathetic tunes to me on his shepherd's pipe. He never harmed me, and only watched, but his eyes burned me like the heat of a hundred suns. Then Hermes came again. He said, "We can still do you small favors, Io." Then he waved his wand over Argus and lulled him asleep and cut off his head. Then a swarm of flies swooped for the head as it floated down river. Suddenly, the flies swerved and turned on me. I see them always before me and behind

me now, beautiful and stinging . . . Oh Zeus, I am
blinded by your splendor spread out before me like a pea-
cock's tail with a hundred eyes! . . . I shall never stop
running. Prometheus, tell me where I must go, and how far
I must run before I die.

FIRST VOICE

Speak to Io, Prometheus.

SECOND VOICE

She wants to know if she will bear a child to Zeus.

THIRD VOICE

She wants to know if she will die.

PROMETHEUS

You will bear a child and you will die, Io, but not until you
have encircled the earth many times. Do not ask how many.
Long before I have finished talking, you will feel the first
false pangs of childbirth. They will mean nothing, but you
will want to be off, and you will even despise me for standing here, and think my patience and helplessness are cow-
ardly indolence. Your child's birth is a long way off, but you
will rush madly from this rock. As if you were meeting it,
you will head into the rising sun. Your one wish and purpose will be to run against the sun. At first, you will hope
to overtake it and catch it, while it is still weak and red and
unable to clear the earth. Later, you won't care much. In
your frenzy, you will laugh at the sun leaping up at you, as
you think, and trying to drag you down, and forever forced
to let you escape. Soon, however, you will come to a crum-

bling plain, as chalky, dead-white and honey-combed with holes as the wastes of the moon. You will run over this plain, until you can remember nothing else, and yet you will see less change than I see from this rock. You will think you are on the moon. Then suddenly, the earth with all its colors and changes will burst on you. You will rejoice in the peoples of the earth. First, you will come to the Scythians, poor nomads and savages, but contented, ingenious creatures, who live in houses they fashion from green branches, and set on wagons. Each wagon-wheel will be as tall as a man, and when the wheels begin to roll and creak, you will think an orchard or a vineyard is rushing toward you, and rustling its leaves in the sunlight. Do not come near these people. Behind each bough, there will be a man with a drawn bow. Oh do not be angry, Io, if the Scythians shoot a few hurried arrows at you. They are poor and must protect their simple houses. Then you will come to the Chalybeans, no nomads or peasants, but builders of cities, and workers in metal. Do not come near them. Their metal work is mostly weapons. And do not be angry, if the Chalybeans fall into a phalanx, and begin to maneuver. They have jealous neighbors, and built their cities with great cost and labor. You will see monsters. You will see the Amazons, angry women, who live without men or children, and build their pinched wooden barracks in the cold shadow of a mountain. Do not fear them. You can come near them and trust them. These women hate men. They will lead you around their mountain. You will have to keep up with hard steps, and yet you will weep when you leave them, because they will have left you with far different women, the three daughters of Phorceys. These will have the bodies of swans, scales covered with feathers, three bodies with one tooth and eye between them. Fear this tooth. But why should I go on talking to you about monsters. When you have seen one, you have seen them all. They are as strange and fatiguing as the whims of the gods.

10

What will I come to next, Prometheus?

PROMETHEUS

Then you will reach . . . Oh what? I have forgotten, perhaps, after ages, you will come to the plains of the moon again. You will see that the River of violence now runs across this land like a scar. Men will be running toward this river . . . they won't be monsters, there will be none left on the earth then . . . no, these will be people, who are more gaily industrious and disciplined than their neighbors, people who have forced every land and water to be a highway for their daring, who imagine they have left imperishable monuments for good or evil behind them—they will be men who hold elections, and know how to obey. These too, when you see them, will of course be soldiers, but more like a broken herd than a healthy army. Driven by thirst and repeated defeat, they will break ranks and crowd into that exhausted river. They will be so close-packed, they will cut one another with the weapons slung under their arms. They will stumble over their abandoned baggage. Other armed men, much the same, and speaking the same tongue, will stand on the high opposing bank, and pelt this herd with spears and stones. The men in the river will not look up, or pay any attention, or try to defend themselves, as they go on lapping up the mud, now dirtied with their own blood—each man fighting and ready to kill the man next to him for a mouthful of that filth.

IO

Will they destroy themselves?

PROMETHEUS

Thousands and thousands will, but some will live. They will be sold as slaves and sent to the rock quarries. There, they will discover that the city they were building and improving is a quarry.

IO

Can I go to the quarry? I pity these men.

PROMETHEUS

No, they will be guarded. The sight of you would fall on them like a shadow. Any interruption or distraction from their work would kill them.

IO

Who can I help?

PROMETHEUS

No one . . . Oh Io, I wish there were time to tell you about the peoples of the earth, and the goodness and greatness they have been given! Do not be angry and call on Zeus to avenge you, if they do not show this goodness, and only draw their swords. Remember you were loved and abused by God. Such women . . . Men are so uncertain, and on edge, and frightened . . . they would kill you.

FIRST VOICE
What kind of god is Zeus?

SECOND VOICE
If his love can only frighten, why is he stronger?

THIRD VOICE
What do you see, Prometheus, when you look at Zeus?

PROMETHEUS
I used to see unending circles of light, gentle, supple, airy, living, and forever widening. But now I see a thunderhead, a false face, blackened, crisp, all-powerful. In the forehead, sensitive blue veins are still trickling, as they harden. Blood turns to metal.

FIRST VOICE
Because we do nothing, Zeus is powerful.

SECOND VOICE
Zeus sits in an armory of power, all force at his fingertips, but he himself . . . he is not powerful.

THIRD VOICE
Perhaps Zeus is soft and hesitant, like the horns of a snail peeping out from its shell.

If I could break that shell, I think I would feel free to yield.

Zeus yielded to me. Will I bear him a son?

Yes, Io, at the end of your journey, you will bear Zeus a son. He will smile on this son, and this son's sons for many generations. Then a daughter will be born to them, the loveliest child ever born. And Zeus will yield to this daughter, as he yielded to you, Io. She too will bear Zeus a son, the finest of his sons. And because this son is the finest, Zeus will yield to him not as a god yields to a woman, but as an aging earthly father gives way to a stronger son.

A child will be born to me. Even if I die, my gentle acceptance will live on in my son, another life, then many others.

Io, this life, the life your son must live, a life you will not live—how will you be able to leave it? I will not speak about that birth, it will be like other births. Your life will be going from you, even before the last pains of childbirth have left you free to feel worse pains. You will not be frightened then, when you wake, and feel a faint, warning breathlessness, then turn to feed your child in the sheltering dark of that first night. But soon, too soon, the night will be torn off you like a dress. Then brilliant and exposed, and wildly gulping the killing air, you will see your nakedness, but you will not admire your sick body with the excited wonder of the god, your lover. You will look blankly into your child's blank eyes, just opened, and already hurt by the light of the sun breaking across the muddy shallows of that dismal little Asian backwater, where he was born. Your eye will be on the distance, you will not see things close to you, or feel how close the air is becoming. You will only listen with terror for the buzzing of the flies, not near yet, their inaudible anger and poised prongs, still strangely withheld, hovering elsewhere, and stopped in the distance, a minute, and then another minute as if the sun had stopped. But the sun's bleak circle will burn, and go on climbing. You will wade out into the water, try to cool yourself, and try to hide your body. There, sinking up to your thighs in mud, and standing still a moment, you will feel, for almost the last time, the hollow heaviness of your body, now freed from your child. You will sink like a waterlogged bough into that sulphury cow-pond. You will be happy to breathe its dead stagnation, and glad that sluggish mists are enclosed and calmed by cliffs, like water stopped by the sides of a cup. Water spiders will slow and clot on the thick syrup of your shadow. The sandpiper that snips at the sandlice hopping between its toes, will skitter toward you on the little black strings of its legs, then pause, as if paralyzed, and peer at you with the beady eyes of a rat. Your child will stare up at you with the same eyes. As you hold your child above the languid black ripples, one taking the place of another just like it, without danger, without sound, almost without change—each ripple no greater than a line on the surface

—you will see that your child's smile has become the smile of Zeus, your old lover, grown wizened and clinging, two red strings at your breasts. Io, the weight that dragged you down will be a lifted burden. You will rejoice, you will feel your milk ebb out of you without resistance, and change before your eyes to the blood of your child, as if the sun had stopped, as if you could rest there from wishing to live.

IO

Will this be my death, Prometheus?

PROMETHEUS

No, you will not rest there, Io. By then, the flies will have found you out. They will see with delight that you are waiting for them, unable to move, and stuck to your thighs in mud. They will sigh over you like a forest of holly, but they will bring no protection, they will give no respite. When they smell the sweat and fear streaming from you, their buzz will rise to a scream, they will quickly alight on your body, swim there—black slime that sticks to you and stings. Then you will start to move. The flies will leave you. The mud will fall off you, and splatter your child, as you hurriedly drop him on the shore, the soft top of his head propped on a stone, his fat feet kicking the water. You will run faster than you ever ran before, but more peacefully now, as if you know the flies would never catch up, that now you had only to fight off the death-stings of your own body, that hound-pack of affliction, closing in to kill you, poor bleeding hound, your tongue dripping, your teeth snapping, the fur of some animal darting before you, grizzled white mixed with the red hairs, like the beard of

Zeus, but no face there, no flesh, only a force dragging you forward to your death, a power so empty, so tireless and so cruel, it could only come from God. Your lungs will tear like worn cloth. The wind will rise, and strike you in the face. You will not think of love then. You will hear tall trees crash at your heels, waves thud against the muddy shore behind you, your child's cry of desertion rise above the waves. You will pass everything you ever passed before, but you will see nothing, you will distinguish nothing. Your eyes will be a filmy glaze. And when you come at last to the talking oaks of Dodona again, you won't understand anything they are trying to tell you, sighing and dying, the black droppage of the leaves falling on your back and splotching like flies. You will run out into the purifying sun. You will stand on the edge of a blazing river. Fish that eat men will snap at your shadow. You will not dare put a foot in that water. You will search for your crossing, as if your life depended on it. You will not be put off by the rocks, as blinding as diamonds in that light, or lose your way in the meanders of that gnashing river, coiling back on itself, like a snake, then suddenly frothing to extinction, thousands of feet, to find its pool at last, its mouth, bronze-colored, spade-shaped, a snake's head part salt water, part fresh. You will see glassy, brown vegetable bubbles, taller than trees, and bloating in that calm, as if they were waiting to catch and swallow the fish. The fish will float guts upward, sawlike gills, dead, still poisoning. You will know then that this is at last the passage, the crossing, that you were always headed for, and that you are never to cross. Each advance toward death will be as familiar to you as a lesson learned by heart. Each step will be a step already taken. And then you will reach the tip of a little point of mud, stop there, and watch the scattered stones of passage lift clear of the water, like the knobs of a whale's spine, and you will stare at that tip still lifting, water rushing down its sides, now rising like a mountain range, land pushing back the waters of the earth, and swallowing. Then Io, if you put your hand to your forehead, you will feel that your hand and forehead are rushing water. Retreating pebbles will leer up at you from the bottom—false coins. Your blood will be draining out. Everything, the dead fish and even your drowned flies, will be going out and away—ebbing, eddying, gurgling, muddying, and grinding together in the soup of that whirlpool. Oh Io, this life, the life you will not live, all its lines will be crossing, entangling, strangling. Your lungs will only give you a trickle of breath, as thin as the clear thread of a spider. Your breath will stick like a cork in your mouth. Nothing will be moved, no life will be fed by your lungs flapping, puffing up, and collapsing on that air—a last breathlessness, the taste of death, if death has a taste. Then Io, you will understand the far-seeing vision of the gods who formed man's body from mud and their own breath—formed you too, to die, Io, a woman standing on that point of mud, on the brink of the helplessness you came from . . .

IO

I cannot speak, I cannot hear you, I cannot stay. (*She rushes screaming off the stage*)

FIRST VOICE
Io is gone, Prometheus.

SECOND VOICE

While you were talking we could almost see her living through her death.

THIRD VOICE

We were living through our own.

FIRST VOICE

We think you were living through your own death, if that were possible.

SECOND VOICE

Giving Io something to hope for would have been more practical.

THIRD VOICE

Why are you looking so angrily at us?

FIRST VOICE

We haven't driven Io away. *We* haven't deserted you in your time of loneliness.

PROMETHEUS

I was trying to feel my way toward truth. One word led to another. Each one might have hit on something that would have helped Io. I myself might have been helped. No, don't check me, I have little faith now, but I still look for truth, some momentary crumbling foothold. Even here, I am too hurried, I am like a pebble caught in a landslide.

The truth, the truth, Prometheus!

That's all we hear about here.

We can't live on such a shadow.

Has anyone ever known the truth, or really wanted to?

No, I don't think so. Or perhaps long ago . . . I forget now . . . I think I may have either known or hoped for something once . . . I forget when though. I remember hunting for. . . what shall I call them? Causes, knots, heads of action? I was a savage head-hunter then, always hot on the trail of powers I hoped to defeat and tame and put to work. I never saw one. I saw nothing, except some hole, light through some eye, some eye that wasn't an eye, but the eye of a needle, forever withdrawing and narrowing, and winking derisively. Everything was held in the grip of something else. I was on a fool's errand, and yet I was guided by the great gods of that day, their most powerful flashes, and later by the steady light of my own mind. That mind was in no way walled in or useless. Each thought was like a finger touching, tampering, testing, and trying to give things a little of my bias to alter and advance. I never felt bound to keep anything to its original custom, place or purpose. I turned the creatures on their heads, and lifted the doors from the hinges of determination.

FIRST VOICE

You never felt bound, Prometheus.

SECOND VOICE

You have left us broken and in the cold.

THIRD VOICE

And yet you *are* bound!

PROMETHEUS

I wasn't alone in my search. There were many others. Zeus himself did more than any. Soon a new world, one of our own shaping, lay on top of the old flat table. This world was more delicate, and reasonable, and worthy of our minds, though perhaps as confused and dangerous as ever a few miles down. Oh do not think I was alone, or that we ever, even at our maddest, abandoned the discoveries of our fathers. We followed them slavishly. If you look closely, you will see that my father, Uranus, the first unerring, though lumbering and short-winded power, has everywhere left his crude footprints on the path here. And now, when I have lost the path, and stand here, even now I think back with delight on those years I gave to puzzling out some footprint, or accident. I would sit by the shores of the ocean. The tides came and went. I didn't see them. I hardly saw the back of my hand, or heard what was said to me. Yet I both saw and heard. I saw to some purpose.

FIRST VOICE

To what purpose, Prometheus?

SECOND VOICE

Surely Zeus had something better in mind by then.

PROMETHEUS

I imagined that each new thought was another upward step on my circling road. To no purpose perhaps. No step reached a landing, no piece of knowledge ever quite turned into wisdom. Zeus gave up. In the end he knew that nothing would satisfy his famished appetite.

FIRST VOICE

What else could Zeus do?

SECOND VOICE

You should have aped his example.

PROMETHEUS

Perhaps, perhaps, but one learns to trust no one, not even God's self-interest. I think I should have been more loyal to the idiocy of things, or bolder, or more careless. Yet I had no choice, such was the gravity and devotion that drew me on. Now I stand fixed and nailed to a narrow frame, to a rock, but I cannot unwish a single minute I clung, transfixed and trembling, to the great frame of being—awed, absorbed, and stunned! Even here, something stirs in my heart. I feel hunger and passion tingle through my outstretched hand. Around some bend, under some moving stone, behind some thought, if it were ever the right thought, I will find my key. No, not just another of Nature's million petty clues, but a key, *my key, the* key, the one that must be there, because it can't be there—a face still friendly to chaos.

FIRST VOICE

You carry us with you, Prometheus.

SECOND VOICE

We too are searching and reaching.

THIRD VOICE

Yet the day for such discoveries is gone.

FIRST VOICE

We would rather be stung by Io's flies than by your thoughts.

PROMETHEUS

You can thank your Father for your lowly birth. I was born higher and had less chance.

FIRST VOICE

If we had been chosen by Zeus, we never could have resisted. All our lusts are eased by the hand of power.

PROMETHEUS

Why don't you leave me? Go, follow Zeus. You are not bound.

Anyone can be dazzled by Zeus. We are more ambitious now. We search and scavenge after a success the world has overlooked, your crooked and oppressed nobility. Stubborn as you are, you know one thing. You know that intelligence is suffering. The other great powers are animals.

PROMETHEUS

Zeus warms his hands at a greater fire than mine. He sits in the heaven of his assurance and our folly. There, the wings of birds never reach him, he is hidden from the other gods, and is free to play with his thunderbolts, each day another sublime crash of fireworks, another mountain range broken beyond repair. His brilliance blinds, his greatness whirs in his ears. He has no time to look down and smile on the slaves who work for him in the depths. He sleeps through the submissive bird-song of their praise. And yet he wakes, and rejoices whenever one of these slaves and obedient instruments is caught on the wheels of his perfection. Do not think Zeus is inhuman and aims too high. He always falls for someone below him. You admire suffering, then admire Zeus. He suffered before he became God, he will suffer again before he falls to nothing.

THIRD VOICE

We don't want to share the fate of Zeus, but we admire him as a ruler. He is the best we've had. How can he fall?

PROMETHEUS

Nothing new. Zeus will fall as they all do. He will fall in love with someone; it will be one of his descendants. She will be dangerous for him to love, but he won't know this, he won't be able to believe it . . . Oh he'll succeed, as he always does with his seductions, but this time he will beget a son, the usual, inevitable son who is always better than his father, a son who will throw Zeus into ruin and forget-fulness. This is my secret. I am not proud of it, it's a thing of no importance. If Zeus were to free me, I think I would tell him the name of the woman. If he keeps me here . . . Well, it won't matter to anyone. Zeus will fall, he will have the leisure of eternity to remember his fathers before him, an infinity of former rulers of the gods, each the be-trayer of his own father, each betrayed by his son. It's the same dull and hideous old story. I fear something much deeper, something I cannot answer.

FIRST VOICE
What do you fear, Prometheus?

PROMETHEUS
I could settle for a succession of gods, each a little stronger and more intelligent than the last. Small loss to us, and some solace . . . All's shining, all stays in motion, the pace keeps rising. Why rising though? Suppose the pace were to slow. No one has ever seen bottom through this life-giving blank. No one will step across the last line of space, or walk back through the atoms and microbes to time's be-ginning. Think of life cooling. No, I think of fire. Fire will be the first absolute power, and the last to rule. Then the trivial order of the gods, that scratch on space, will crackle. Zeus then will be a small flame trickling and dying out

among a million dying flames, that were once alive, were life.

Is this the fire you stole from the gods?

You can fawn on your temporary tyrants all you wish . . . I fear the fire. No, this is Zeus. I hear the low sad moaning of imprisoned thunder. Zeus has heard me. That's how he used to call to me, when he was helpless. He is coming here. I think he is crawling to me on his hands and knees. He will strike away my chains. He needs me. I am ready to speak to him. I think we can trick or at least delay the fire. Our minds will be joined again.

You only hear what you wish to hear. Zeus will never come to this rock. He is sending Hermes, his messenger.

Yes, I recognize the insect buzzing of those winged heels. Hermes is a hard god. He used to be one of the most unimportant. Sending him here was an error. I won't answer his questions. I see through Zeus now, I see the spots of rot on that large forehead. He is so strong, he'd rather die than accept my terms. I too would rather die than accept his. Because of us perhaps. Yes, because of us, the fire is already rising to bury the gods. No one will brush the burning ashes from our backs.

Prometheus Bound

[*Enter* HERMES, *the messenger god and son of Zeus. He has wings on his heels, and a graceful, easygoing way of talking. His words, however, are edged with condescension and an unfeeling aloofness. He only understands authority, and is vexed at having to negotiate with* PROMETHEUS, *who has none.*]

HERMES

The air is fresh and clear on this mountain. I've seen many worse places. Zeus has chosen wisely for you, Prometheus. I hope your thoughts are growing clearer.

PROMETHEUS

Why are you here, Hermes? I have learned that nothing but punishment falls from the heavens. Have you come to torture me?

HERMES

No, no, step forward, Prometheus, step forward. We must talk . . . Oh, I see you can't move. My brother, Hephaestus, is a thorough workman. Rather too thorough . . . he has a pitying, uncertain mind and a hand of rock. If I had been in charge of fastening you, I wouldn't have pitied you, but I would have left a little loose chain for you to swing on. The clinking of your fetters would have been like sheep-bells on this mountain-top.

PROMETHEUS

Are you going to release me? You speak without anger, but I feel as if I were already enclosed in a rotting darkness.

HERMES

You misunderstand my duties. I cannot release you. I have

no thunderbolt to blast you loose from your rock. I am a light and sunny god, who is afraid of thunder. I can only talk. Zeus has often sent me to talk to his women. This mission is more difficult.

PROMETHEUS

Are you really alone? Am I alone with you? I thought Zeus . . .

HERMES

Zeus won't come here. Don't stare off into space, as if you expected him to drop from a cloud. You are experienced in his affairs. You know Zeus can't be everywhere, but he follows everything. If things go badly between us, I am the last god who will ever come here. Try to look me in the eye.

PROMETHEUS

I see the eye of my accusing judge. I think you intend to be heard, but you will not listen.

HERMES

Unfortunately, the gods can't trust you, or treat you any longer as an equal. You have done things. You are an outlaw. I haven't come to talk about that.

PROMETHEUS

I have done things. I have helped Zeus. Am I beyond the law because I helped God?

HERMES

From now on, what you do, and how you do it, and when you will do it, must be left to Zeus. You must become as obedient and dependable as a star. Perhaps, we'll let you shine as brightly. No more stealing fire from the gods! That was lawless. Man wasn't helped. If you could look down on the earth from this rock, you would see man's blackened trail of motion. I haven't come to talk about that.

PROMETHEUS

Why are you troubling me?

HERMES

You made a prediction, a very off-hand and desperate one. Your suffering makes you see everything through a yellow and crooked glaze. Still, the gods must follow up every clue. You said Zeus would over-reach himself. Something about a woman. She would bear Zeus a son . . . I can repeat your exact words; you spoke of a son who would throw Zeus into ruin and forgetfulness. Give me the names of that woman and son.

PROMETHEUS

A prediction? Don't think about predictions, Hermes. Even when they are true, they are dangerous. The suspicions of tyrants create the usurpers they fear. Often they have speeded their own fall, and rooted out whole houses and dynasties, because of some desperate prediction. I won't join in that man-hunt.

HERMES

You must hunt with the gods, or be hunted down and torn to pieces.

PROMETHEUS

They have already run me down. No matter what I do, I will be torn. I would be more desperate than I am, if I trusted the savagery and hollowness at the core of power. Oh to be young again . . . you are like new-born wasps, already swooping through your sunshine, already on the scent of blood. There are birds in the air.

HERMES

Birds?

PROMETHEUS

Each hungry throat will be swallowed by a larger and emptier throat. That's the law. I've seen too many high gods crash from the still sky.

HERMES

We are as fixed as the sun and stars.

PROMETHEUS

No, there's no foothold on your heights. You are already on your way down. Your fall will be hard, your fall will be soon. This golden and almost eternal reign of Zeus, what is it? Something as bright and stony and momentary as the sun. Zeus is a spot in the eye of chaos . . . Poor, little new god, you'd better scurry home to your father. He couldn't even teach you how to ask the right questions. He is afraid to understand his own loneliness and danger, though he is still on his throne, and still walled in by his indifference. The indifference of his subjects is greater. Rulers always fall, but no one cares much, except the ruler.

HERMES

You cared once, Prometheus. Remember how you groaned over the old gods. They were pretty sad material for their duties. A hundred fussy, grasping hands for every task, nothing ever done quickly or cleanly. You were the first to rush in and help Zeus throw them down. Even then you were too rash, you hardly understood the responsibilities of power. You had to be thrown down yourself. And now you seem to stand on tiptoe in your chains, still criticizing, offering improvements, and ready to answer questions you've never been asked. Zeus does well enough without you. The world has never been better. Of course, there are still a few shadows. You must tell me how Zeus will over-reach himself. Come, speak out, don't put me off with your usual dark riddles.

PROMETHEUS

Now that I am chained here, I suppose I am almost free at last. You look on me as an insect, but you can't harness an insect like an ox and force it to haul your cart of stones. I won't answer your questions.

HERMES

You are still stating your terms to Zeus. He can't accept any. Don't you understand how weak and unimportant you have become? The strong have always done what they are able to do, and the weak what they must.

PROMETHEUS

If I am unimportant, why do you threaten me?

HERMES

What I ask of you is quite likely slight, but your defiance is grave. The gods cannot honorably pass over disobedience. I will tell you what is going to happen to you. Zeus is about to break this rock with his thunderbolt. You were expecting as much perhaps, but you may have thought we would then forget you, and leave you standing here, still able to breathe this clear mountain air. But there won't be any *here* then, there won't be any mountain, only a smolder of crumbling rock falling with you, only you yourself crumbling and choking and tearing yourself apart on the sharp descending fragments of rock. You will fall longer than you have already lived, and you will have time as you fall to relive in thought every second of your obstinate life a thousand times.

PROMETHEUS

How ignorant you gods are! You think you are standing still. Your feet and mine are sinking in the same drifts.

HERMES

No, you must not flatter yourself, or imagine that Zeus is willing to let you float downward into oblivion forever. You are not subject to the kindly laws of decay. Zeus will drag you back here again, and expose you again to this blinding and inquiring daylight. Never again will the day-light seem like something joyful and accustomed. Your chains will be heavier then, your flesh will be weaker. Nothing else as weak and quivering will be left alive to suffer. No friend will recognize you, none will want to. And yet there will be one creature, and only one then, who will still take notice of you and hope to draw profit. Yes, your eyes are returning to that creature, it's that spot in the distance. You are wondering whether it is truly a spot, or just a wound in your eye. Prometheus, the spot is out there waiting, and it is also your wound. It is the vulture of Zeus. When you return to this rock, the vulture will join you, an uninvited guest at the banquet. The banquet will be *you*. Thin pickings, you might think for such an appetite, but the vulture will feast contentedly without pausing on you, and tear your flesh to ribbons, and dip his crooked, butter-yellow beak in your liver. Each morning, your liver and innards will be as red and firm as the bald red head of the vulture, each evening, they will be as black and dead as mud. The vulture will never consume you—each night your slashed flesh will slowly and painfully heal, your liver will regain its natural colors. Do not expect your torture to grow less, or even worse—that would be allowing you too much variety. Each new pain will be an endlessly antici-pated repetition; the sufferings of one day will be the sufferings of the next. Once nothing was as quick and changeable as your thought, Prometheus, but if Zeus thinks on you at all in your latter days, his meditation will be mo-notonous, blocklike, and crude. Do not imagine that any god will drop from the sky like a bird and offer to take your place. No grateful mortal will wrench himself loose from his burial and offer himself. Neither you nor anyone else will kill the vulture. Zeus himself might be killed as easily. When you stare at the vulture's red head in your misery and wickedness, Prometheus, you will perhaps think of the heart of Zeus. This is the heart we have given God.

PROMETHEUS

Hermes, you too will be drowned in the blood of that raw heart.

HERMES

No, not yet. I can still give you a minute or perhaps two minutes to answer and submit.

FIRST VOICE

Submit to the gods, Prometheus, submit to the gods!

SECOND VOICE

We dare not tempt their malice. Do you see how Hermes, one of the least hateful, is gloating when he speaks of your torture?

THIRD VOICE

Hermes gloated, and yet we think his offer is good.

SECOND VOICE

No firm promise, a small gray hope—you have nothing to lose.

FIRST VOICE

Perhaps Hermes' life will even be a kind of hope for you.

See how well he lives, how freely he flashes through the sky, dodging every disaster, following his own wishes, and the gravity of power.

SECOND VOICE

"This is far from freedom," you'll say, "or even life, unless our lives are no more than the life of a stone or a star."

THIRD VOICE

We don't know how to counsel you.

FIRST VOICE

No, we believe it's reckless and dishonorable for you to want to break your neck on this rock, on the hand of Zeus.

PROMETHEUS

I have decided, I have chosen. Look, children of the Ocean, you and I and Hermes, and all the gods and Zeus himself, who is chained to the quarry he terrifies . . . we are all beginning to slide on our thinning downward thread. All standing here, all descending, all standing here again, we will be stopped, blocked, frozen in our suffering. And below us, perhaps, there will be creatures who are even lower, and they will go on and on, giving birth and dying. Each death will be a conquest. What kind of a conquest? Who knows? The air I breathe is like a metal bucket. The creatures are like sheets of soft lead, unmoving but seeming to ripple in the water-circles of the bucket. The gods too, though they are too perfect to change or die, they will be like a sliver of quicksilver blindly circling and circling on itself in a bucket. God then will be the only creature, free to be both motionless and alive, a mirror freed at last from all reflection. And yet he will not be free. God will feel the withdrawal of the creatures, see his own death there, and know that he himself must die before our suffering can end.

HERMES

Come, birds of the sea. I already hear the thunder rolling a little. The sky is like a bowl about to crack and break. The destruction of Prometheus is beginning. Zeus wouldn't like for anyone to stay here and share his fate. You mustn't watch Prometheus suffering, or even know it will happen. Zeus himself would rather not watch or know. Yet he must always watch and know. He must swerve and follow the course of his nature. He is not permitted to toss away his power, give ground, or nod. If a creature doesn't give way to him, Zeus must strike that creature. If the creature fights back, Zeus must strike twice as hard. That's the law. Come!

FIRST VOICE

We will go with you, Hermes, we must obey. What else is there? We wanted to escape with our lives from life. (*Exit* HERMES, *followed by all the* BIRDS. FORCE *and* POWER *appear and stand behind* PROMETHEUS)

POWER

We've reached the end of the road, the topmost stone on the rooftop of the world.

FORCE

Beyond here, everything is downhill.

[*Increasing darkness, lightning, thunder.* PROMETHEUS *and his rock begin to sink and disappear.*]

PROMETHEUS

That black cloud is moving toward me. It's as hard as sheer rock. Soon my voice will be lost in the sound of breakage. I no longer can see Force and Power. No, there in the squirls of lightning, I see Zeus. His hands are not tied. I am burning in my own fire.

Oh Earth, my holy Mother, look, you will see us suffer.